I0472627

# The 2011 Top Ten Obstacles To Project Success

*By: MüTō Performance Corp.*

Written by: Lou Gasco

Edited by:  Mary Kay Massey

Compiled by: The MüTō Team

# Table of Contents

# THE TOP 10 OBSTACLES TO PROJECT SUCCESS

## The Original Card Game for Project Professionals

### SUGGESTED RULES OF PLAY

## HOW IT STARTED:

Every project ever attempted has been plagued by at least one to three of the Top 10 Obstacles to Project Success. Some project professionals are lucky, and get to deal with ALL TEN on a single project.

Our company has made it an annual process of surveying the Global Project Professional Community to find out how frequently these obstacles affect their projects. Over 6,000 professionals have participated in our surveys since 2009.

Part of our process is to cull through the best practices being employed by those who are *not* experiencing the obstacles, to understand how they detect, assess and mitigate them from occurring.

Our clients benefit from this research when we consult them on how to best mitigate obstacles from affecting their project. Their Project Professionals benefit from the methodology we invoke through trainings, and hands on experience as our *Project Specialists* employ the MüTō Method™ to successfully guide projects already in motion past these obstacles.

## *WHY THE GAME?*

One day, in discussion with a youthful group of pre-teen project manager hopefuls, we were discussing the Top 10 Obstacles, and they decided it would be a good game.

We thought it would be fun, kitchy, kooky idea.

During some off-hours (not many) we designed the deck, and then during one of our 2nd Thursday Networking events we showed it to a few people. We were amazed at the reception!

"This is my project!"

"I have these obstacles!"

"Huh? That's an interesting Idea…I have to try that on my project."

Were some of the responses when people saw the cards, or played the game.

Then it hit us. This would be a GREAT WAY to teach Project Professionals about the Top 10 Obstacles! How to mitigate them and what they can do to a project.

And by gosh, it was time for Project Managers to have a game all their own!

What follows is the rules we came up with….feel free to invent your own. One of our customers uses the cards as TAROTS to fortell what will happen to their next project. (I can't verify or deny the foretelling power of the card, but the revelations were UNCANNY!)

# ENJOY!

PS. If you have Questions, comments, suggestions….(especially if you have any ideas for surreptitious behavior) feel free to contact us at INFO@MUTOCORP.COM

## ▲ *PREPARING THE GAME*

0. You need a playing surface. We recommend a table with a few chairs. Four players seems an ok number, but Two can have a quick bout of fun.

1. **The Pile:** Remove all six instruction cards, (PREPARING THE GAME, GAME PLAY, GAME END, OBSTACLE CARDS, MITIGATION CARDS, and SUBTERFUGE CARDS), shuffle the deck and place it face down on the table within reach of all PM's.

2. **My Project:** The space in front of every player will be known as their "Project." Time Chips, and active cards go here.

3. **Choose the length of game.** # of Time Chips needed to end a round and # of points needed to win the game. **We recommend FIVE Chips be the length for a quick fun round about 20 minutes.**

4. **Draw your hand:** Each player takes turns drawing cards privately from the Pile, until all players have five cards in their hands.

## ▲ *GAME PLAY*

**Game play starts.** *(The first player is the one with the least project management certifications...if there is a tie, and then the one with least pm experience goes first.) Each player takes a turn as follows;*

**A. Take a Time Chip; add it to your project.** *(AS SOON AS YOU REACH THE LIMIT SET ABOVE, THE ROUND ENDS!)*

**B. Draw a Card from the pile; show it to the other PM's then do what it says under the section marked DRAW.**

**C. Play a Card; (this is Optional.)** *Some cards have a PLAY instruction; these can be PLAYED to improve your project, someone else's (for you good Samaritans) or to damage a project.*

**D. True-up.** Discard into the bottom of the Pile or Trade away any cards you have. You can't have more than five in your hand at the end of your turn.

**E.** The next player repeats the above steps until the round ends.

---

✱ *Discuss how the mitigations that have resolved your obstacles might have really worked, or how unresolved obstacles would have affected your project, and you'll be learning/preparing for the next obstacle that hits your project! (think of it as a fire-drill.)*

---

## ▲ *GAME END*

*The round ends as soon as a PM has the required number of Time Chips (as agreed on step #2. in Preparing the Game.)*

*The PM starts out with a score for the round of 5 points. They subtract a number of points for every unmitigated obstacle. (Note: the PM may actually wind up with a project that scored negative points; oh well, you an still throw a success party!)*

**Play another round until a PM reaches the agreed upon Points needed to win the game!**

**Check out OBSTACLE, SUBTERFUGE and MITIGATION instruction Cards for information on each card type.**

*We welcome your suggestion for*
*SUBTERFUGE cards. They help spice up*
*the game and lend the realism that makes the*
*Top 10 Obstacles unique to each*
*organization.*

### VISIT OUR GAME-BLOG AT

http://TheTop10ObstalcesGame.Wordpress.Com

Or Scan our QR code

# *Forward*

What follows is the result of an annual effort. Thousands of Project Professionals from around the world participate, and provide us with their feedback not only during the time of the surveys, but also during our conferences, seminars and speaking engagements.

When data is derived from so many sources we run the risk of getting a meaningless pile of information that doesn't really point to any particular common denominators. Gladly, this is not the case here. As you read on, you'll be thinking about the times some of the events described occur on your projects, and how similar some of the characters appear to ones you know.

We are confident that you will see the reality of your projects in the coming pages. Not every situation will mirror your own, and not every obstacle may apply, but our hopes are that somewhere within, you will find at least one gem of shared experience that may help you with one of your future projects.

We thank project professionals around the world for sharing their thoughts through our surveys, and our families and friends for putting up with our obsession.

But most of all, we thank the reader, for sharing your time with the product for our labor.


Sincerely,

*The MüTō Team*


*PS. A personal note of thanks to Mary Kay Massey who labored the many grueling hours to help get the writer's technicaleese to something understandable by human beings ☺*

# Introduction to the Top 10 Obstacles to Project Success 2011

At the beginning of the New Year we invite global participation in our annual survey on the *Top 10 Obstacles to Project Success*. In

1. Changes to Project Scope (Scope Creep)
2. Resources are Inadequate (Excluding Funding)
3. Insufficient Time to Complete the Project
4. Critical Requirements are Unspecified or Missing
5. Inadequate Project Testing
6. Critical Project Tasks are Delivered Late
7. Key Team Members Lack Adequate Authority
8. The Project Sponsor is Unavailable to Approve Strategic Decisions
9. Insufficient Project Funding
10. Key Team Members Lack Critical Skills

addition to ranking their top 10 obstacles, this year we also captured data about the types of projects, industries, and geographic region.

More than 1,700 respondents took the survey representing 22 industries, 26 countries and 47 types of projects. Over 63.6% of the respondents worked in the U.S.A., 9.1% in India, 5.5% in United Kingdom, and 3.9% in

Canada. Over 20 other countries represented 17.9%.

Regionally, 67.5% of the respondents were from North America, 14.8% from Western Europe, and 11.7% from the Middle East and Southern Asia. South America, Asia/Pacific, and Eastern Europe represented 6%.

A wide variety of industries were represented, the top five included, Information Technology (29.2%), Financial Services (19.3%), Consulting (13.6%), Pharmaceuticals (6.6%), Healthcare 5%, Training/Education (4.4%) and Manufacturing (4.4%). Seventeen other industries represented 17.5%.

Our respondents were involved in a variety of projects. The top five types of projects were New Application Development (28.9%), Infrastructure Implementation (11.4%),

Process Optimization (9.0%), Marketing (6.4%), and Construction (5.1%). Over 40 other project types represented 39.2%

Our survey asked respondents to provide information about the frequency of occurrence of each obstacle on their projects. We used a rating system to interpret the responses to the survey. A frequency of "100% of the time" earned a rating of "5", while a frequency of "0%" earned a rating of "1." This rating system provides insight about the obstacles that are more of a concern than others, how that concern has changed since last year, and what the risk of experiencing any particular obstacle on a project may be (frequency of occurrence).

| The Top 10 Obstacles to Project Success | 2009 | | | 2010 | | |
|---|---|---|---|---|---|---|
| | Ranking | Rating | Frequency of Occurrence | Ranking | Rating | Frequency of Occurrence |
| Changes to Project Scope (Scope Creep) | 1 | 4.13 | 83.6% | 1 | 3.17 | 48.2% |
| Resources are Inadequate (Excluding Funding) | 3 | 3.91 | 73.7% | 2 | 3.08 | 41.0% |
| Insufficient Time to Complete the Project | 2 | 3.95 | 77.8% | 3 | 2.90 | 34.0% |
| Critical Requirements are Unspecified or Missing | 8 | 3.49 | 50.3% | 4 | 2.83 | 36.0% |
| Inadequate Project Testing | 4 | 3.69 | 60.8% | 5 | 2.70 | 30.9% |
| Critical Project Tasks are Delivered Late | 5 | 3.70 | 59.6% | 6 | 2.64 | 24.9% |
| Key Team Members Lack Adequate Authority | 6 | 3.69 | 59.6% | 7 | 2.63 | 26.1% |
| Project Sponsor is Unavailable to Approve Strategic Decisions | 9 | 3.27 | 39.2% | 8 | 2.41 | 26.9% |
| Insufficient Project Funding | 7 | 3.53 | 53.8% | 9 | 2.40 | 22.4% |
| Key Team Members Lack Critical Skills | 10 | 3.32 | 33.9% | 10 | 2.55 | 22.5% |

The global results indicated that the top three obstacles are still the same. *Scope Creep* still rules supreme as the **#1 obstacle to project success**. *Resources are Inadequate (Excluding*

*Funding)* edged up above the obstacle *Insufficient Time to Complete the Project* to take 2nd place. *Key Team Members Lack Critical Skills* kept a firm hold in 10th place. However, *Insufficient Project Funding* has dropped to 9th from 7th place. Interestingly, a lack of funding does not appear in the top three obstacles even though the world is suffering from a global recession.

The results revealed some anomalies. The first to catch our attention was the obstacle *Critical Requirements are Unspecified or Missing* jumped from 8th place in 2009 to 4th place in 2010. This was the largest change in the ranking of any obstacle. When we analyzed this dramatic shift we took a look at the top four obstacles, and found a cause and effect relationship between obstacles 2, 3, and 4. If *Resources are Inadequate (Excluding Funding)* there

will be *Insufficient Time to Complete the Project.*
When project teams realize this, they tend to
economize and overlook small details which
result in *Critical Requirements are Unspecified or
Missing.* This is one possible hypothesis. In
the months to come we will focus our efforts
on understanding the reasons for the new
rankings.

The next interesting anomaly was the fact that
each obstacle occurred with less frequency in
2010 than in 2009, meaning the overall ratings
have dropped. What created this trend? In
order to view this drop more accurately we
normalized the data. We placed a
comparative of the rate of occurrence from
2009 and 2010 in order from lowest to
highest. The drop in ratings of both years
was both universal and early identical.

This pattern would indicate that project managers have been universally influenced by a global trend. One could surmise that the world's project management capabilities have significantly improved. Although obstacles occur, they occur with less frequency overall. Our respondents might also be reacting to the impact the global recession has had on their project environments. Perhaps the global recession has caused us all to focus on mitigating problems more seriously because the impact of project failure could be more severe. Project managers are clearly doing more with fewer resources.

When we ordered the overall rating by obstacle and graphed it, we found that two of the obstacles did not drop as far in frequency as the others did. The obstacles *Resources are Inadequate (Except Funding)* and *Critical*

*Requirements are Unspecified or Missing* appear more resistant to the universal trend causing the overall drop in frequency. This suggests that the cause of the universal trend might also be fueling these obstacles. We might modify our prior example as follows; the global recession has caused many companies to lay off employees, this has resulted in the obstacle *Resources are Inadequate (Except Funding)* to occur. As a result, there will be *Insufficient Time to Complete the Project.* When project teams realize this, they tend to economize and overlook small details and as a result *Critical Requirements are Unspecified or Missing.*

Every project in 2010 experienced an average of two to three of the top 10 obstacles. Each project was at risk for at least one of the top three obstacles. With an estimated \$12 trillion spent in new projects globally last year, \$4.8 to

$8.3 trillion risked failure from one or more of the Top 10 Obstacles. Although a drop in frequency has occurred, project failures still exist with staggering financial impact.

The regional data revealed interesting similarities and differences. Respondents in North America, Western Europe and Middle East/Asia held that *Scope Creep* belonged in the top three. Respondents in Western Europe relegated *Resources are Inadequate (Excluding Funding)* to 9th place, while North America and Middle East/Asia put it in the top three. Instead, Western Europe placed *Key Team Members Lack Critical Skills* in 3rd place, while the other two regions put this in 9th and 10th place. North America and Western Europe agreed that *Critical Requirements are Unspecified or Missing* was among the top 3, but Middle East/Asia voted this as less of a problem than *Critical Project Tasks are Delivered Late.*

There's no doubt that the geo-political landscape and global financial recession has had its share of impact on the Top 10 Obstacles to Project Success. It's interesting to note how *Insufficient Project Funding* should be rated low, but the shortages of resources and times to deliver projects are rated high. The reoccurring #1 obstacle *Scope Creep,* reflects an inability on the part of organizations to head off trouble before it impacts projects. In an ideal project environment processes are used effectively and automated systems make them less onerous. Every project team member communicates clearly with each other, while each member is highly motivated. All project tasks are processed with complete accountability by responsible parties. We are clearly not there yet.

# What is Scope Creep?

## *Obstacle #1: Scope Creep*

The respondents to the *Top 10 Obstacles to Project Success* have reported that *Changes to Project Scope (Scope Creep)* occurs on half of all projects. *Scope Creep* comes up in almost every conversation about a project gone badly or in complaints by project team members about a project's condition. *Scope Creep* is the scapegoat for most of the troubles on projects. Our analysis showed that although ranked highest among the *Top 10 Obstacles to*

*Project Success*, the commentary provided indicated that the meaning of *scope creep* is interpreted in many different ways

Here are a few comments that illustrate the point;

- The catch-all phrase and primary definition we received is "Any requirements added late in a project." This definition classifies every new requirement as *Scope Creep*, without regard for either the source of the new requirement, or its applicability to the project.

- Some described *Scope Creep* as "Any time the business (the sponsor or beneficiary) wants something they simply add it, and it's usually at the worst possible time." The business is blamed for continuously adding requirements in a haphazard way.

- "Legitimate needs require legitimate changes to the scope of a project." This definition indicates that there is legitimacy to *Scope Creep*. Many respondents went so far as to comment that change occurs naturally on a project, and must be accounted for in planning.

The majority of our respondents interpreted *Scope Creep* as changes made to project requirements that affect or change the original intent of the project. All agreed that the obstacle was created by the fact that project team members had to redesign the project while it is underway. The most exciting element of the analysis is that two distinct perspectives exist. Some respondents claimed that *Scope Creep* is legitimate, while others thought exactly the opposite. Both camps agree the impact of *Scope Creep* is the utilization of resources that are otherwise employed. The material difference between the two is the way scope creep is introduced to a project.

*Legitimate scope creep* is a change to a requirement that is based on a legitimate event. For example; the company has just declared a merger and the project must now change in order to accommodate the new addition.

*Illegitimate scope creep* stems from a want or need of a sponsor or beneficiary that is inconsistent with the goals of the project. For example, the project is a new product launch. The beneficiary is the manager of the customer services department. The original requirements for the project include some automation of customer services processes. The beneficiary requests that all of the department's processes are automated, and not just the few that pertain to this project.

By examining the project manager's role and actions as they relate to the causes of scope creep, the difference between legitimate and illegitimate becomes a bit clearer. A project manager should not stand in the way of a legitimate change in a project since it is intended to support necessary changes to the business strategy. If there is any question to the legitimacy of a change requested by a beneficiary, the sponsor can provide validation for the change. Of course this becomes more complicated when the sponsor is the requestor of the change. Once approved, the project team must support the change with every effort, as they would any original requirements.

When an illegitimate change is not stopped early enough the project team will spend time and resources analyzing, designing, implementing and testing it. A project manager must always be able to explain how a change is helping the project support its business strategy. If they cannot, a project team will start to feel the strain of the additional effort with no understandable purpose and it will impact their abilities.

A misinterpreted form of *Scope Creep* can be found when a significant requirement is missed during design. For purposes of this discussion, this is defined as an *invisible requirement;* a requirement that existed all along but was missing or unspecified until later in a project. *Critical Requirements are Unspecified or Missing* is significantly different in cause and mitigation from *Scope Creep* that it appears on the *Top 10 Obstacles to Project Success* as a different obstacle.

*Scope Creep* occurs so often that a project manager should expect to be approached by his sponsors or beneficiaries to add some requirements mid-way through the project. As a best practice the project manager should assess the request in order to ascertain its legitimacy. If the legitimacy is questionable, a project manager must discuss the requirement with the requestor to understand the effect it will have on the scope of the project. The requestor would have to explain why the project should use its resources to process the scope change. If they cannot do so, the project manager knows he is dealing with an attempt to promote *illegitimate Scope Creep*.

All *illegitimate Scope Creep* must be prevented from occurring otherwise it will impact the project negatively. Our analysis showed that when *illegitimate scope creep* impacts a project, the project manager is either forced to accept the change by some higher authority, or lacks the capabilities and resources to prevent it.

*Scope Creep* no longer sounds creepy when it is caused by a legitimate need. Projects will undoubtedly be challenged by the full specter of *Scope Creep*. If it is anticipated it can be ushered through appropriately, and projects will be made all the better for it. *Legitimate Scope Creep* will not damage a project unless it is mishandled or treated as though it were *illegitimate*.

◆

# Did We Let Go of the People We Need?

## Obstacle #2: Resources are Inadequate

Given current events, it's interesting to note that the obstacle known as *Resources are Inadequate (excluding funding)* has risen in rank from #5 in 2008, to #2 in 2010 on our annual survey of the Top 10 Obstacles to Project Success. Results indicated that for every five projects initiated, two were impacted by this obstacle.

In the current global economy many companies have been forced to reduce their labor resources through lay-offs. Companies using lay-offs as a strategy to control costs, put their project based investments at risk. Simply put, these projects no longer have sufficient skilled resources and risk successful completion.

This obstacle existed in our 2008 survey before significant layoff activity occurred. This indicates that the *Resources are Inadequate (excluding funding)* obstacle is not exclusively driven by the state of the economy. The reason a lack of funding is excluded from this obstacle is due to the difference between non-financial and financial resources. Even if a project is well funded there may not be enough non-financial resources to adequately support a project's successful completion. Money may not be the solution for a skilled labor shortage, unavailable infrastructure or a logistical delay in raw materials.

By the time the resources are recognized as being inadequate, the impact of the obstacle is already occurring. Timelines are missed and stress rises when project teams are forced to do *more with less*. So why then would organizations knowingly put their new business initiatives at risk by getting rid of more people?

The environment may be such that a project being undertaken is so important to the survival of the enterprise that there is no other way but to risk its failure by overburdening the project with inadequate resources. "Better to have tried and failed, than never tried at all." This approach is best described as a last ditch effort.

The risk of failure in some cases may be so high that one would question the viability of the project to begin with. This is a highly charged topic, and generated commentary from across the spectrum of project team members including project sponsors, beneficiaries, and project managers. Project managers accustomed to doing more with less are now being asked to do, "Much more, with much less." Project sponsors generally accept that a viable strategy is to cancel projects in order to free-up resources for other more needed projects. This strategy is met with increased resistance in the current economic climate because resources have been cut more dramatically and there are fewer projects that can be cancelled without detriment to an organization's overall business strategy. As a result last ditch efforts seem to be par for the course.

The imperative is for project managers to determine from their sponsors, whether their project is a last ditch effort or not. If so they must focus on completing the project while mitigating the risks involved when *Resources are Inadequate*. However, if they find that the project is not critical to the survival of the organization, they may help their sponsors by making a case for the cancellation of their project. The redistribution of the cancelled project's resources can then help critical projects succeed. Of course, suggesting that a project you are managing be cancelled may put you on the list of potential lay-offs, which is the conundrum.

# So Little Time, So Much to Do!

## *Obstacle #3: Insufficient Time to Complete the Project*

Over the past three years one of the interesting changes in the results of our annual Top 10 Obstacles to Project Success Survey has been the movement of the obstacle *Insufficient Time to Complete the Project*. In 2008, our respondents ranked it as obstacle #8, in 2010 our respondents voted it obstacle #3! The portion of respondents identifying it as an obstacle nearly tripled. None of the other obstacles changed its ranking as dramatically over the same period of time.

There may be many reasons why this obstacle is critical, and some may seem obvious given the 2010 business environment. Some respondents commented that they were pressured by their sponsors for quicker recovery of their ROI, others by their beneficiaries to gain benefits sooner. A third group of project managers claimed that they would run out of resources due to cost cutting unless they finished their projects sooner than expected.

Project managers and their teams have always felt the pressure to finish projects on-time. It is an expected component of the roles and responsibilities of their respective jobs. Project managers usually hear a triad of complaints, "Not enough time, not enough resources, and not enough money."

Almost all of the project managers we polled interpreted the obstacle in the same way. The pressure created by the project's challenging timeline negatively impacts the quality of the project's outcome. According to standard project life cycle methodologies the date of delivery of a project is a function of the project's planning process. The date estimated for completion of a project is agreed to by consensus of all of the project's subject matter experts, project managers, sponsors, and beneficiaries. Our analysis indicates that project teams are creating this obstacle for themselves by accepting pressured rather than optimum timelines.

Survey responses revealed that project teams rarely have the opportunity to consider an appropriate delivery time-frame. More often than not, the date of delivery is assigned to the project. Sponsors and beneficiaries tend to assign pressured delivery dates as a requirement for success. Rather than setting an appropriate timeline, it appears that project teams are being ordered to finish projects by an inadequate date.

The cooperative engagement between project team members, sponsors, beneficiaries, suppliers and project managers with respect to the date of delivery of a project, has become a rare event. Completion dates on projects are now dictated to project teams by the sponsors and beneficiaries. This may be a result of the rise in the do-or-die nature of organizational strategies. In any case, the date of completion of a project has become a *requirement*, often one that does not get processed with the same due diligence as a true requirement should.

# When One Assumes

## *Obstacle #4: Critical Requirements are Unspecified or Missing*

Of the *Top 10 Obstacles to Project Success* the obstacle that creates the most finger pointing is *Critical Requirements are Unspecified or Missing*. Respondents to the 2010 survey commented that one out of every three projects suffer from either a partial or complete lack of critical requirements. The occurrence of the obstacle on their projects was blamed on the lack of analytical skills necessary to identify requirements. Some blamed the beneficiaries for not knowing enough about what they wanted, while others blamed the suppliers for not knowing better.

An interesting attribute of this obstacle is the way it appears on a project. Typically, the obstacle does not become obvious until suppliers start wondering how they are going to accomplish specific requirements without some extra work involved. The need for extra work becomes evident from an emerging fact that a critical requirement is clearly missing. For example, let's say supplier (A) has to deliver requirement (X). In order to do so she needs requirement (Y) to be completed. So she asks supplier (B) when he will finish requirement (Y), supplier (B) responds, "What is requirement (Y)?"

There is a general lack of subject matter expertise amongst the suppliers involved in this scenario. This leaves other project team members to wonder how supplier (B) missed such an important requirement, or how supplier (A) could have properly estimated their participation in the project. These questions are valid however, when we analyzed the nature of missing requirements we noted that they usually consisted of small elements that most suppliers and beneficiaries take for granted. Respondents commented that their beneficiaries believed the suppliers should have known the unspoken requirement was necessary, in most cases the suppliers felt they were not at fault.

Sponsors are usually left out of the picture, finding out about the missing requirement only when they are asked to sign off on a change control. In many cases, sponsors are left wondering why the requirement was not part of the original estimate and project design. Since there is usually still time to save the project they tend to authorize the change control.

Sometimes the obstacle does not appear until the beneficiaries are asked to accept the final results of the project. At that point beneficiaries usually refuse to accept the project as complete, and suppliers are asked to deliver the missing requirement. Suppliers typically respond that they were never informed of the requirement, and beneficiaries usually fall back on the rationale that the supplier should have known better.

Ultimately, a decision is made to either include the missing requirement and delay the project, or exclude the requirement and complete what is left of the project on time.

Excluded requirements are typically added to a list of things that have yet to be done after the project is finished. Many respondents described requirements grouped into projects with titles such as "Day 2, Day 1.2, or Day 3." Although each of these constitutes a separate project, technically they are part of the original project and its objectives. The inevitable delay caused by the completion of these subsequent projects could have disastrous effects on the strategic objectives of the organization.

Beneficiaries are responsible for dictating the set of requirements needed to complete the objectives of the project. When a *critical requirement is unspecified or missing*, inevitably fingers point in the direction of the beneficiary. Many of our respondents commented that assumptions are made at the moment of requirement definition. The rest of the project team assumes that the beneficiary knows enough to provide complete details on all of the requirements necessary to fulfill the project. Likewise, the beneficiary sometimes assumes that the suppliers know enough to fill in any blanks that they may have missed.

In some cases, both the beneficiary and the supplier are assuming the other party knows what is required to do the job. It's apparent that these assumptions occur more often than not when we consider that this obstacle occurs on one out of every three projects. Armed with this knowledge, project managers are in a great position to do something about it. Whether or not they join a project in its earliest phases, the project manager can gain a clearer understanding of the requirements, the objective of the project, and what suppliers are delivering. By matching all three to each other, clues to assumptions which may have been made will start to appear. These clues will help the project manager identify whether or not those assumptions are linked to some task on the project. If they are not, then the project manager has just brought visibility to an unspecified or missing critical requirement with sufficient time to do something about it.

◆

# Why test?

## *Obstacle #5: Inadequate Project Testing*

Respondents of MüTō's survey on the Top 10 Obstacles to Project Success reported that one out of every three projects experience *Insufficient Project Testing*. What makes this obstacle unique is that its impact is felt after the project solution is in place. The solution does not satisfy the needs expressed by the project and must now be repaired because something went wrong. In other words, what was a project is now an emergency.

The phase in which the repairs take place now occurs after project completion. Old resources, if still available, are called back in or new resources are quickly put into place to figure out what happened and fix the problem. This leaves any casual observer asking whether the problem that occurred could have been detected earlier in order to avoid the embarrassment (and job insecurity) this type of event causes. The answer is yes, but only with proper testing of the project's solution at the appropriate time throughout the project.

The term "testing" typically engenders resistance by most sponsors as they wonder why they are being asked to set aside upwards of 30% of their project funding to test whether the subject matter experts have erred in the implementation of their project. The first question a sponsor will ask is why so much? This is usually answered with charts and tables that prove that finding a problem in an earlier phase of a project inevitably costs less to correct than finding it later. The second question, typically born out of frustration, is directed at the subject matter experts and suppliers; if they knew what they were doing, why test? If the suppliers and subject matter experts do their job correctly, the 30% allocated for testing could be reduced to a much more comfortable 5%, or even eliminated altogether.

This question, "why test," usually causes upheaval in a project. There is a fundamental conflict between the approach the sponsor and the project manager take when resolving this issue. The project manager is left without an adequate response when a supplier's expertise is questioned. From the sponsor's perspective they are paying for perfection, not imperfection. From the planning perspective, project managers must prepare for the unknown as a necessary element of design, including a supplier's potential error.

When the sponsors question the subject matter experts and suppliers about the limits of their expertise, the SME's and suppliers tend to reinforce the fact they know what they are doing, and are not likely to make any real mistakes. Those responsible for testing are forced into a position of having to prove just how overconfident the suppliers and subject matter experts have been. Testers often resort to pointing out prior failure rates to question the expertise that is being touted to the sponsors by the suppliers, and SMEs. This gets the testers involved in a 'he said, she said' type of argument. Testing may be reduced to a point that's less than optimal for the testers depending on the ability of the suppliers and SME's to convince sponsors that they will not make any significant mistakes on this project.

Testers often explain their cost estimate and efforts on a project by using best practice examples and industry accepted statistics. This distant understanding of industry best practices does not bear weight to a sponsor who feels versant on their project and is comfortable with the expertise of their suppliers and SME's. Sponsors assert that the entire testing effort on their project is something the industry is forcing them to do as a best practice and does not address the fact that they are paying their suppliers to be perfect. Sponsors argue against the imposition of what seems to be no more than a "30% testing tax."

The pressure to complete the project begins to weigh heavily into the equation and inevitably those responsible for testing are viewed as the obstacle to project completion. Some will argue that they do not need testing because it offers little value and serves to slow a project down. That is a bit like saying that preventative medicine is a waste of time because all that is needed is some good invasive surgery once one is stricken with a disease. Others may argue that testing is the equivalent of placing much needed resources into prevention for something that may not even occur.

When a project is not considered critical to the organization's strategy, correcting post-implementation problems may be possible. When the project is critical, fixing problems after implementation may have dire consequences to the organization. The need for testing is directly correlated to the criticality of the project.

Applying generalities to the diverse topic of testing assumes that testing is a single event occurring at one time in a project. When we analyze the topic of testing we find that there are multiple testing environments and phases associated with a project. To explain this distinction, we have categorized the subject of testing into three arenas.

In the first arena testing is accomplished by the supplier or subject matter expert and is sometimes called Acid Testing. This testing is usually completed behind the scenes and not specifically accounted for as testing on any project estimates but bears a material role in the project's outcome. Acid Testing is typically performed to review whether a deliverable produced by a suppliers or SME is complete and within their own satisfactory levels of quality. Some suppliers have complex processes to complete Acid Testing, while others conduct only the cursory reviews. The budget for Acid Testing is typically included within the supplier's own estimates for producing the deliverable. If Acid Testing is ineffective in any way, the next opportunity to catch the error in the deliverable is during Quality Assurance Testing.

Quality Assurance testers make certain the aggregate set of deliverables on a project falls within a range of acceptable quality. When all the deliverables are gathered from the suppliers, QA Testers make certain that the deliverables are what project sponsors paid for, and beneficiaries ordered. If the suppliers are not doing their level of testing effectively, these QA Testers will do extra work. QA Testing may reveal the failures caused by suppliers that have conducted inefficient Acid Testing prior to delivery.

But testing does not end here. There is another area of testing that is typically completed by the beneficiary. Some call it End User Testing, others Acceptance Testing. When the beneficiary receives the completed project he must accept it as the finished product by testing it himself. If he finds anything wrong at this stage all hell breaks loose. QA Testers are the first to get questioned, with the suppliers in close second. At this point the cycle of project repair begins.

Our survey respondents have indicated that projects with insufficient testing are usually discovered by the beneficiaries. This reinforces the importance that testing should occur not only at the end of a project but throughout the project at various stages in its development. If the appropriate testing is not completed effectively throughout the project the ramifications can be profound.

When the QA Testers attempt to collect their 30% tax, sponsors ought to have a conversation before accepting. They should find from their project managers if suppliers are adequately tooled to accomplish their own Acid Testing. If they are not, then it is clear that the costs of QA Testing will be driven higher. Project managers can reduce the QA Testing tax by holding suppliers accountable for completing appropriate Acid Testing. Sponsors should never reduce testing unless they wish to place the project at risk for failure or the project is not critical to the strategic goals of the business.

# "It will just take two weeks!"

## *Obstacle #6: Critical Project Tasks are Delivered Late*

Many people who have hired a supplier to provide them with a deliverable have been given an enthusiastic promise such as "It will just take two weeks." The time comes and goes, and either the deliverable goes unmet or problems arise. When the supplier is asked for a new ETA, the response is often "I just need two more weeks." Respondents of the *Top 10 Obstacles to Project Success Survey* indicated that one out of four projects had *critical project tasks delivered late.*

The risk of project task delays is commonly mitigated through the use of what is known as a "buffer." The way a buffer works is that project managers add an additional period of time over their supplier's estimate to account for potential late delivery. This buffer is accumulated at every step of an estimate and usually amounts to a significant figure on a project. Many of our respondents reported buffers from 30% to 100% above their supplier's original estimates. For example; a project that was initially estimated by suppliers to take from four to six months, now takes nine months with all the added buffers.

The problem is that business depends on projects to succeed. The use of buffers indicates that the project manager does not know how long the project should take. Bear in mind that subject matter experts and suppliers give estimates of completion based on their expertise. By definition, adding a buffer onto estimates demonstrates that expertise is in question.

It gets worse. Remember, one out of four projects have added buffers and still receive deliverables late. Perhaps they did not include enough buffers? Perhaps the length of each buffer should have been doubled? Tripled?

We investigated further and found that regardless of the amount of buffers put in place on a project plan, late delivery of tasks by suppliers prevailed. The reasons suppliers are late had less to do with time allotment than with management best practices. We grouped the reasons for late delivery into three primary categories;

- **Unclear communication of requirements:** suppliers find it extremely difficult to deliver on tasks successfully when they do not understand the requirements.

- **Upstream suppliers delivering their tasks late:** although this is the same issue compounded, it happens so often that it deserves its own category.

- **Inadequacies in the supplier's processes and methodologies:** this could be as simple as poorly estimating the time required, or as complex as a lack of processes and methodologies in place to assure on-time delivery.

The project manager is well positioned to handle all of these categories. However, it requires considerable effort and an increased level of interpersonal communication skills. For example, when the beneficiaries and suppliers meet to discuss project requirements, the project manager should facilitate discussions to confirm that the suppliers understand the requirements as the beneficiaries intended. The project manager will be able to make certain each requirement has been answered by a supplier's detailed estimate. If needed the project manager may call on a Subject Matter Expert for support in understanding the supplier's detailed estimates. The SME can confirm that the estimates can support the requirements.

A Project Manager can use the dependency of one supplier to another to improve the accountability of the upstream supplier for on time delivery. Rather than sitting back and waiting for the supplier to report completion, the project manager should track major milestones that are better defined than "task start" and "task end." This knowledge forewarns a project manager of issues and helps them mitigate the risk of late delivery. This exercise makes time estimates more accurate.

If the supplier is unable to provide major milestones, it is a clear indication that they lack either process or expertise. This is a red-flag to the project manager and serves as a definite indication that the estimate of time cannot be trusted. Replacing the supplier with a more proficient one is a preferable mitigation strategy. In most cases, this is not an option, especially when the supplier is part of the same department or organization sponsoring the project. If this is the case, an SME could help a project manager understand the details by reviewing the estimate with a supplier. The project manager facilitates this review and any lack of expertise will be revealed as the supplier rationalizes their estimate. Frequently, a supplier in this situation gains clarity into their own processes and modifies their estimates as a result.

Relying on the use of buffers to mitigate the risk of late project delivery is clearly not a project manager's best option. When the project manager facilitates the estimation process by bringing beneficiaries and suppliers into agreement, or by helping suppliers with SME's, they take an active role in mitigating the risk of late delivery. Doubling or tripling the buffer is a poor second to holding a supplier accountable for their estimate.

◆

# What's my job?

## Obstacle #7: Key Team Members Lack Adequate Authority

The briefing with the sponsor went well for our project manager. The sponsor delineated the goals of the project, the proposed budget and the proposed timeline. He even told the project manager who his suppliers were going to be and which of the internal associates were going to be the beneficiaries of the project. Then he said, "Now go, manage the project but before you make any major decisions, come see me."

Our project manager approached his suppliers and introduced himself by saying, "I'm the project manager so don't make any decisions without me." The suppliers let their teammates know the same. The beneficiaries emphasized they were in fact the authority on the project since it directly benefited them, and it would be okay for the project manager to come to them for approvals.

Unfortunately, this story is all too familiar. Respondents of the survey on the *Top 10 Obstacles to Project Success* reported that a quarter of all projects are impacted by the fact that *Key Team Members Lack Adequate Authority*. Based on the diversity of the comments we received about this problem, the above story just begins to scratch the surface.

To better describe this obstacle, we have categorized the comments we received into three variations;

1.  Project team member's roles and responsibilities are clearly defined, but their authority to carry out those responsibilities is insufficient.

2.  Two or more project team members have clearly defined but overlapping authority, roles or responsibilities.

3.  Project team member's roles and responsibilities are not clearly defined.

The first variation is most apparent with suppliers but also occurs with every key member on a project team; project managers, sponsors, and beneficiaries. The obstacle occurs when a project team member is required to accomplish a task, but cannot complete it without outside intervention. If they have no authority over the outside entity there is no way for the project team member to guarantee the completion of their own task.

When the project beneficiary lacks authority the acceptance of project results is delayed. They cannot carry out the acceptance without a superior's approval. It is rare that a beneficiary's superiors must be involved in the approval process, but when it occurs, progress can be grossly impeded. Often they are not versant on project nuances. Delays can come from the time required to bring the superior up to date and manage misinformed objections.

The scenario so commonly reported that it might be better described as the nature of the job rather than a project obstacle, was the one in which the project manager accepts the role of managing the project with extremely limited authority. In every case, when *Key Team Members Lack Adequate Authority* to carry out their responsibility there will either be delays as the proper authorities are sought, or a lack of quality as the project team's stress rises from frustration.

When more than one project team member is delegated the same role and responsibility it is usually the sponsor and beneficiaries that overlap. The project sponsor benefits from the completion of a business strategy which may involve more than one project. The beneficiary benefits only from the completion of the project. When a project team member is both the beneficiary and the sponsor of a project the tendency will be to favor the project, and not the business strategy. When a project sponsor and beneficiary serve reverse roles on competing projects the tendencies will be for each of them to support their own sponsored project, and not each other's.

Another scenario is when a central supplier is relied upon by many other suppliers. That central supplier is treated as a pseudo-beneficiary whose needs eventually overshadow those of the true beneficiary. Other suppliers depend on the central supplier for the interpretation of requirements, and subsequent decisions are made without the true beneficiary's input. Project delays ensue as confusion over the requirements grow, putting the project at risk.

When a project manager struggles to hang on to their authority because a sponsor, beneficiary or supplier has hijacked it, the project team is challenged with trying to determining who is actually managing the project. Questions that need answering are not asked, and decisions are delayed in their execution jeopardizing project quality and completion.

It's not easy to detect when a project team member's role, responsibility and authority is not clearly defined. From the perspective of the individual involved, they believe they know their role, responsibility and authority as given to them. They can easily detect when their authority is insufficient but they have a hard time understanding when their authority overlaps someone else's. When a project team member has not been given clearly defined roles, responsibilities and authority, they cannot perform their tasks adequately.

A project supplier has the most far reaching, negative impact on a project when they do not know their role, responsibility and authority. They will estimate the wrong effort, and produce the wrong deliverable. In most cases, the deliverable they provide will be some shade of what was desired but not entirely appropriate, and will likely be rejected by the beneficiary. With any luck it will be close enough that the beneficiary can live with it, and the negative impact to the overall business strategy it supports will be minimal.

Only slightly less common is the case in which the beneficiary does not understand their total role and responsibility on the project. Many respondents have commented that their beneficiaries behave as the worst prima-donnas, ignoring any responsibility on the project other than accepting the eventual deliverables to their liking. This phenomenon is so common it has become widely accepted as the norm, and in some cases is imbedded in the culture and project life cycles in many organizations. In truth, the beneficiary's role and responsibility is so much more than this. Best practices and common sense dictates that in order to accept the deliverables the beneficiary must be able to clearly understand them and test them. Suppliers must have discussed the requirements with the beneficiaries to determine what the deliverables ought to be. The beneficiary's role, responsibility and authority on a project includes acceptance of the final product, accountability for the testing of the final deliverables and for the delivery of requirements to the suppliers.

Sponsors sometimes misunderstand their own roles, responsibilities, and authority. Our respondents claim that some sponsors acted as an omnipotent presence on the project, while others simply served the function of funding the project like an anonymous benefactor. The sponsor that acts as an omnipotent presence interferes in the authority of other project team members. It is possible that they do not understand their role, responsibility and authority correctly. The anonymous sponsor is not available for sponsor decisions.

Sponsors fund the project and have authority over funding decisions. They also reap the benefit from the success of the organization's strategy once the project is complete. This is vastly different from the beneficiaries of the project who directly benefit from the outcome of the specific project, and indirectly from the organization's strategic success. Any major decision on the project which may impact the overall business strategy must be reviewed and accepted by the sponsor. No one else on the project may do this. Some sponsors feel that this may be beneath them after all they have hired people for the very purpose of making decisions. It is possible in these cases, that the direct sponsor of the project is only a proxy for some other sponsor. Sometimes finding the true sponsor for the project requires detective work. It is important to understand the nuances of the sponsor hierarchy so that a project manager may appropriately escalate decisions and mitigate risks that may ensue.

This brings us to the project manager. The role, responsibility and authority of a project manager generally reflects both the best practices of managing a project life cycle, and the management of a team of people. Some of our survey respondents defined their role, responsibility and authority in a way that reflects one or the other but not both.

The best practices of project life cycle management are necessary and often differ from organization to organization, or project to project. The project manager must have an in depth familiarity with project life cycle management and the nuances of the best practices being used on the project by the organization. Without this knowledge he risks poor communication with his project team, or worse, applying the wrong life-cycle management technique at the wrong time on the project. For example, a project manager that attempts to manage a project using a strict sequential project life cycle with a project team that has studied and practices the Agile Methodology will get his head delivered to him at the first Scrum. This project manager will insist on full disclosure of all requirements when in fact, the Scrum is an incremental process for discovering requirements.

The best practices of project team management define the project manager's ability to interact with his project team. He uses these methods to communicate clearly, motivate them, and establish accountability. A project manager who has a good grasp of project life cycle management but cannot communicate clearly, motivate his team, or hold them accountable will be less than effective. These skills become tantamount to the success of the project any time the project manager is called upon to handle an emergency. For example, when faced with potential *scope creep* the project manager must be able to facilitate the vetting of the proposed change, and will likely have to do so in the face of mounting political pressures. Their relationships and ability to communicate with the sponsor, beneficiaries, and the subject matter experts will be critical to a successful vetting discussion. Another example is a project manager that is faced with a supplier who is tardy in delivering their task. Their ability to hold that supplier accountable will become more important than the project life cycle.

There are a number of variations to this obstacle and differing perspectives to examine depending on the project team member involved. If roles and responsibilities are misunderstood due to poor communication or improper planning, there is no way for authority to be set effectively. If authority is not set to match the proper roles and responsibilities project team members will not be capable of controlling their own output. This decreases the chances that the project will achieve its successful conclusion, or worse, leaves success completely up to chance.

◆

# Where'd they go? I thought I saw a Sponsor?

## *Obstacle #8: The Project Sponsor is unavailable*

For as much as project managers would like it to be true, sponsors cannot be counted on to be available whenever a project manager needs them. According to the *2010* survey on the *Top 10 Obstacles to Project Success* one out of every four projects is impacted by *Project Sponsor is Unavailable to Approve Strategic Decisions* at some point during the project. This becomes an obstacle to project success only if the sponsor is missing at a critical moment. The success of the project is often at risk in these moments.

Many of the respondents to the survey attributed this obstacle to the sponsor's lack in understanding their role and responsibility. Others blamed the course of normal business for pulling sponsors away from projects. An analysis of the responses indicates that *Project Sponsors Are Unavailable to Approve Strategic Decisions* due to a combination of both.

For example, there is no such thing as a certificate of sponsorship, or a BBA degree in project sponsorship. Unlike many of the other positions on the project team, subject matter expertise is not required of a sponsor. By definition a project sponsor is someone who is financing a project with the goal of accomplishing some overall organizational objective. Unlike beneficiaries, sponsors do not benefit directly from the outcome of a project, but rather from the impact a project or group of projects has on the organization's overall strategy. Many respondents reported that their sponsor's act as if they completed their role and responsibility on a project by signing the check that funded it. In this case, a problem arises when they are not available to handle their other role, which is to be the sole authority on critical project decisions.

This can happen for a number of reasons. Project sponsors tend to be senior people within an organization. They may be called away to other organizational requirements such as; a board of directors meeting, a crisis in another area under their management, client meetings, sales meetings, or the occasional management training. These events are common place, especially in most large organizations. The multiple non-project related roles that sponsors have tend to redirect them to areas other than those that require the project's success.

The inherent risk to project success becomes clear when we take into account the likelihood that the sponsor will disappear due to some natural business event. Knowing this in advance helps a project manager plan against this risk. Depending on his relationship with the sponsor and ability to communicate, the project manager can mitigate the risk by simply asking, "Who do I get approvals from if you are not around?"

When a sponsor is needed and cannot be found projects can stall. Decisions get delayed. Small issues often grow into large disasters, and windows of opportunity to correct issues are lost or become unnecessarily rushed. In these situations many project team members will take it upon themselves to make the decision on the sponsor's behalf. Beneficiaries and suppliers will try, but for the most part it is the project manager who takes on the role of *pseudo-sponsor*.

Our research shows that there is a direct correlation between the frequency of a *Project Sponsor Who is Unavailable to Approve Strategic Decisions* and a drop in project team morale and quality of output. The project manager is not only the care-taker and project team manager, but he is also the link between the project and its sponsor. When a project manager lacks the communication skills to

serve as that vital link, the entire project team
may wonder "Where'd they go?"

◆

# The Trouble with Money

## Obstacle #9: Insufficient Project Funding

The project is ready to start. The concept is sound. It will return great benefits to the company. The suppliers are the best in their field, and the beneficiaries have really done their homework. The sponsor is impressed with the gathering of intelligence, professionalism, and expertise on the project. The same sponsor balks when he sees the proposed budget. He begins to smile, and admits that although this project is likely to save the company, it cannot be completed at the price tag that is proposed.

This is one way projects meet up with *Insufficient Project Funding*. According to respondents of the *2010 Survey of the Top 10 Obstacles to Project Success*, this obstacle affects nearly one out of every four projects. In this case, a project is conceived and planned to perfection but, when all the estimates are calculated, it costs more than the sponsors have budgeted.

Sponsors attempt to prevent this particular chain of events from occurring by making the budget a requirement of the project. For example, they will list the goals of the project and state that they must be reached for a specific amount of funding. The sponsor believes that this will somehow spur the project team into completing the project within budget. However, the sponsor has falsely set his own expectations. In order to complete the project the beneficiaries and sponsors must still come to agreement on the needs of the project. The subject matter experts must analyze the requirements put forth by the beneficiaries, so that suppliers can estimate what they will require to complete all the deliverables. This estimate represents the financing needed to complete the project successfully, but may not be within the sponsor's budget guidelines.

Whether the budget is a requirement or not, if the estimate is higher than the sponsor is willing to spend they will begin to negotiate with their own project team. For example, they will attempt to save money on a supplier's bid for their deliverable by insisting that supplier reduce their cost. The supplier is more likely to reduce either the quantity of his service, or the quality of his deliverable to accommodate the reduction in their profit. In the case of a supplier who is internal to an organization, negotiating their cost is a ridiculous proposition. Unless they are economically profiting from the effort there is no cost factor for the internal supplier to reduce except for the quality of their deliverable. Yet sponsors persist as if they will receive the same deliverable.

There are a variety of reasons why sponsors might act this way. They may be limited in their funding and required to complete a project to satisfy an organizational strategy. If they have no authority to increase funding, they are caught between a rock and a hard place. According to our respondents, this type of situation occurs on one of every two projects. This means that the quality or quantity of the supplier's efforts will be compromised from the very inception of the project.

An external supplier is likely to have included a measure of profit in their estimate. Although there is room for negotiation in the profit, the supplier is more likely to reduce services or the quality of the resources, in order to maintain his profit margin. In the case of an internal supplier, there is no profit therefore, negotiation results in the reduction of the quality of the supplier's deliverable.

A sponsor may also cause the loss of efficiency by selecting an alternate supplier. In this case he finds a cheaper supplier to produce the same deliverable. As long as the cheaper supplier is producing the same quality deliverable, this strategy may work. Many of our survey respondents stated that the supplier originally selected is usually the best for the project, and not the cheapest. The cheapest supplier may be lacking some service that makes them less optimal and reduces their cost. Regardless of the reduced cost, they are not competitive because their service to the project will produce less than what is desired.

Projects also suffer when deliverables are cut out in order to satisfy cost. Cutting deliverables works only when the deliverables are not critical. When critical deliverables are cut, the project will not complete successfully. At times this tactic is used when another project can be funded at some later date which will complete the organizational strategy intended with the original project.

Our respondents claim that project teams are commonly brought in after a budget has been determined. Many reported that those budgets are given an allowance to grow or shrink to accommodate the project team's estimates. The allowance in these budgets has been reported to be as much as 50%. A project budget of $1 million could grow to be as much as $1.5 million. In turn, if this project originally had a rate of return on investment of 15%, the ROI would be reduced to less than 8%. The allowance in project budgets appears to address *insufficient project funding*, however, when considering the overall organizational strategy the allowance only defers the problem.

Some companies have devoted funding for exploring project viability. Less than 5% of our respondents have implemented estimation budgets that allow project teams and sponsors to explore project concepts and estimate overall costs. Organizations that follow this project viability process have less of a tendency to experience *insufficient project funding* than those that do not.

We have discussed how the obstacle appears from actions taken in the beginning of a project. The current global economic recession has a negative fiscal impact on existing projects as well. By definition this is not *Insufficient Project Funding*. Instead, it is another obstacle called *Scope Creep*.

Unlike *Scope Creep*, *Insufficient Project Funding* appears when estimated costs exceed budget.

During the course of a project, should the business environment change, as it does during an economic downturn, any number of events may occur to negatively impact a project. One of them may be a reduction in the budget available to complete the project. The mitigation of this situation is the same as a project impacted by *Scope Creep*, new plans must be designed to complete the project which accommodate the new limitations.

The solution to *Insufficient Project Funding* is dependent on the sponsor's thorough understanding of the estimate derived during the planning process. Is it as optimal as possible? The sponsor can determine whether any further reductions in the estimate will have a negative impact on the project. If the estimate exceeds the budget the sponsor has available, there is really only one choice:

Do not pursue the project unless the project is critical to the organization's survival. Then the sponsor must accept the fact that they have inadequate funding, and risk any number of additional obstacles that will arise as a result.

◆

# They don't know what they are doing!

## *Obstacle #10: Key Project Team Members Lack Critical Skills*

The title of this article is a quote from a senior manager at a major financial institution. He was commenting on the critical skill sets of his key team members in his information technology department regarding their performance on a current project. When questioned further, the senior manager admitted that he did not know what skills the team was lacking, but was convinced that they did not have them. When asked how he could know this, the senior manager responded that he was told by the team that they could not do what was asked of them. At a rather large meeting intended to resolve a problem, key members of the information technology department pointed out that it was not a lack in critical skills that prevented them from completing their task, but rather the lack of appropriate infrastructure. The senior manager responded that there was no funding for added infrastructure and what he wanted now was a solution to the problem. One project manager clarified the issue by saying "You can't drive a car very far without wheels; buy us wheels."

When a lack in critical skills is blamed for a project's problems, it is likely that there is more to the issue. As we saw above, the project team had the skill to understand the problem, but lacked infrastructure to support their solution. It was only at the large meeting that the sponsor realized it was not a lack of critical skills in key team members, but a lack of infrastructure. Respondents of the *2010 Top 10 Obstacles to Project Success Survey* indicated that nearly a quarter of all projects encounter a lack of critical skills in their key team members which prevents successful completion of their projects. Whether there is really a lack, or it is purely a misinterpretation of another issue, it is likely that both are equally responsible for this statistic.

When natural causes such as hurricanes or global economic collapse are not available, many project autopsies seem to point toward a project team member's lack of ability as the cause of project failure. Typically they are made the scapegoat for the project's failure, and never really given a trial by a jury of their peers. In many cases, our respondents indicated that the project manager is usually either the scapegoat, or joined at the hip with the scapegoat. This is because it is appropriately deemed the project manager's responsibility to understand the capabilities of the project team. The project manager must therefore understand and correct the situation before it becomes an obstacle to the project's success.

Understanding why *Key Project Team Member's Lack of Critical Skills* can be blamed for project failure illuminates how an individual's level of capability can impact a project. This highlights the responsibility of the project manager to identify and address the risks introduced by *Key Project Team Member's Lack of Critical Skills*.

By doing so the project manager is armed and ready to counter any witch hunt for a scapegoat that may ensue if a project fails due to some other cause. This knowledge helps him to communicate real issues and their mitigation regarding less than optimal skill sets with the team before they become an obstacle to project success.

The problem is most relevant when it involves the suppliers. If suppliers lack the skills to support their deliverables on a project then the project cannot be completed. Even worse, their deliverables may not be of the quality expected. If realized early enough, replacing the supplier with a more capable one, or supporting the supplier with a subject matter expert or two to mentor them, may be the solution. If realized late, there is almost nothing that can be done other than weather the storm. This would be recorded as a strike against the project manager in the final score on the project's failure.

When the skill set deficiency lies among the beneficiaries, the project is seemingly doomed from the start. Well intentioned beneficiaries who do not truly understand the organizational strategy, or are not capable of expressing what they require from the project, will cause more harm to the project than those who do not know how to fulfill the requirements. They send suppliers on wild goose chases in an attempt to complete their poorly thought out project requirements. They are also not able to appropriately test these requirements when it is time to accept the completed deliverables. When faced with this situation, respondents to our survey indicated that the suppliers are the project manager's best friend. They are the first to say, the beneficiaries "…don't know what they are doing!" It's then up to the project manager to make sure the beneficiaries get the help necessary to complete their task. If the project manager fails to do so, then score another point against them when it comes to rationalizing the project's failure.

However, when the sponsor lacks the skill set to fulfill their role, projects seem to succeed in spite of it. Respondents to our survey indicated that sponsors that are not capable of doing their job become a problem only when they are needed to make major decisions. They commented that the sponsor's best ally and closest advisor in this case is the project manager. This is not to say the project manager is making the decisions on behalf of the sponsor, rather their role is to support the sponsor's ability to make their decisions. This relationship is successful only if the project manager has the ability to establish himself as the sponsor's advisor. If the project manager cannot do this they will have another strike against them when the project fails.

Whether perceived or real, the project manager stands to lose a great deal when a lack in critical skills is to blame for a project's failure. The first part of the solution comes from understanding the source of the skill set deficiency. Once detected, the project manager seems to be the only person who can actually do something to support the key team member lacking the critical skill. Getting the project team member some help from a subject matter expert, or replacing with more capable resources, may be the solution. It is the project manager's responsibility to raise the alarm and promote the adjustment. Otherwise, when all the dust has settled from a project's failure, someone in a position of authority is likely to say "That project manager did not know what he was doing."

# About MüTō

Since 2007 we've been helping Project Management organizations that are experiencing the Top 10 Obstacles to Project Success. We promote best practices and follow stringent detection, assessment, and proprietary consultative methodology to a variety of industries. We look forward to speaking to you about how to mitigate the obstacles that are derailing your projects.

Results of MüTo Performance Corp.'s comprehensive analysis of each of the Top 10 Obstacles to Project Success, the examination of early detection methods, and exploration of mitigation paths will be covered in upcoming MüTō articles and discussion boards available on LinkedIn, and at

http://Top10Obstacles.Blogspot.com/

CONTACT US AT info@mutocorp.com

Or visit our website at
www.MutoPerformanceCorp.com

Or scan our QR Code...

www.ingramcontent.com/pod-product-compliance
Lightning Source LLC
Chambersburg PA
CBHW061512180526
45171CB00001B/152